EXPLORING CONTINENTS

ANTARCTICA

Tristan Boyer Binns

Heinemann
LIBRARY

www.heinemann.co.uk/library
Visit our website to find out more information about Heinemann Library books.

To order:
 Phone 44 (0) 1865 888066
 Send a fax to 44 (0) 1865 314091
Visit the Heinemann Bookshop at www.heinemann.co.uk/library to browse our catalogue and order online.

First published in Great Britain by Heinemann, Halley Court, Jordan Hill, Oxford, OX2 8EJ, part of Harcourt Education.

Editorial: Louise Galpine and Harriet Milles
Design: Richard Parker and Q2A Solutions
Illustrations: Jeff Edwards
Picture Research: Mica Brancic and Beatrice Ray
Production: Camilla Crask

Originated by Chroma
Printed and bound in China by WKT

10 digit ISBN 0 431 09743 7 (hardback)
13 digit ISBN 978 0431 09743 5 (hardback)

11 10 09 08 07
10 9 8 7 6 5 4 3 2 1

British Library Cataloguing in Publication Data
Binns, Tristan Boyer
  Antarctica. - (Exploring continents)
  1. Antarctica - Geography - Juvenile literature
  I. Title
  919.8'9
A full catalogue record for this book is available from the British Library.

Acknowledgements
Alamy p. **27** (LightTouch Images/Colin Harris); Corbis pp. **7**, **9** (Galen Rowell), **11** (John Noble), **24** (Underwood & Underwood), **25** (Ecoscene); Getty pp. **5** (Imagebank), **16** (Taxi), **18** (Art Wolfe), **23** (Illustrated London News), **26** (Aurora); Empics p. **10**; Nature Picture Library p. **13** (Doug Allan); Network Photographers p. **19**; NHPA pp. **15** (Patrick Fagot), **17** (John Shaw), **22** (Rich Kirchner); Science Photo Library pp. **12** (British Antarctic Survey), **14** (British Antarctic Survey), **20** (David Vaughan).

Cover satellite image of Antarctica reproduced with permission of SPL/Planetary Visions Ltd.

Every effort has been made to contact copyright holders of any material reproduced in this book. Any omissions will be rectified in subsequent printings if notice is given to the publishers.

CONTENTS

Words that appear in the text in bold, **like this**, are explained in the Glossary.

WHAT IS A CONTINENT?

The Earth has seven very large areas of land called **continents**. Some are surrounded by oceans, such as Antarctica. Other continents are joined together, such as North and South America. Continents usually have many countries and different peoples living in them.

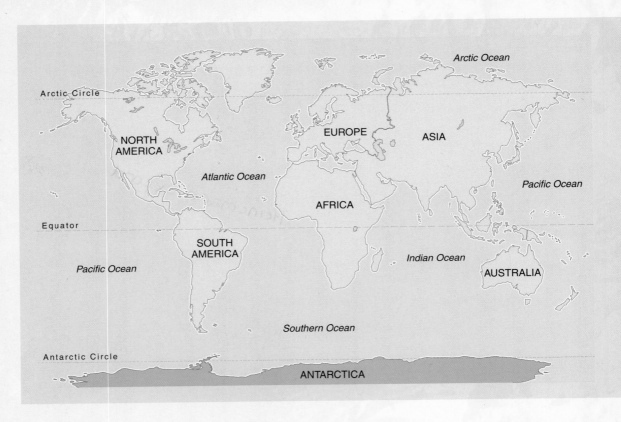

Like nowhere else

Antarctica is different. There is nowhere else like it on the planet. There are no countries in Antarctica. The land is mostly covered by a sheet of ice that is miles thick. Antarctica is too hard a place to live in for very long. Instead, people stay for a short time. They use the sky, land, snow, ice, and water to learn about the rest of the planet. Over twenty-three countries from other continents have **research stations** in Antarctica.

Life in Antarctica

Most continents have different **environments**, with many types of plants and animals living in them. Antarctica is different because it is very cold and dry. Few plants and animals live there. Scientists study the ones that do, because they are very well **adapted** to their cold environment.

Antarctica is the fifth largest continent in the world. It is twice the size of Australia and one and a half times the size of the United States. The coldest and harshest part is the South Pole. As you move further away from the South Pole and closer to the **equator**, the environments become friendlier to life. More plants and animals can survive there.

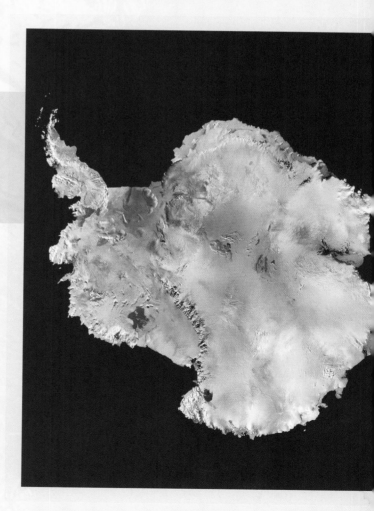

If you look at Antarctica from space, you can see how icy – and beautiful – it is.

Did you know?

Most of the continent of Antarctica is made of rock, but only 2 per cent of the rock is showing. The rest is covered by a sheet of ice up to 2.7 km (1.6 miles) thick!

WHAT DOES ANTARCTICA LOOK LIKE?

Antarctica has land and water like all other continents. But the land is mostly hidden under ice, and the rivers and lakes are mostly frozen or hidden under ice. The ice that covers the continent is called the Antarctic **ice sheet**. The Antarctic Peninsula and islands around the main **landmass** have more rock showing through the ice.

The ice

Antarctica has frozen rivers, called **glaciers**. They look still, but like all rivers they are moving towards the sea – they are just moving very slowly. Glaciers speed up as they reach the coast, when they flow at about 1 km (0.6 miles) a year. Most glaciers flow on to **ice shelves**. When ice shelves and glaciers get to the coast, they break off into the sea as **icebergs**.

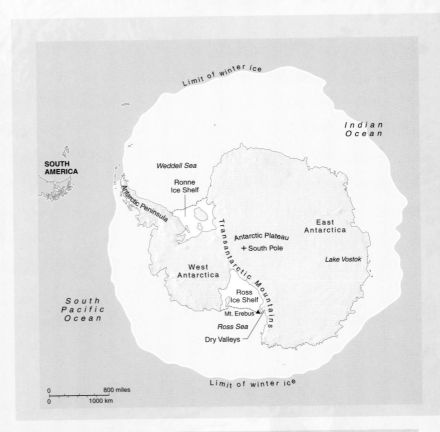

Did you know?

Antarctica is made up of rock pushed deep into the Earth by the weight of the ice. If the ice all melted, the land would slowly spring back up, like a very big cork in the sea.

Icebergs

Because icebergs are formed with freshwater, they float on the salty seawater. There are different types of icebergs. Most start off as **tabular** icebergs. These are shaped like big tabletops. As the iceberg melts, its shape changes.

Lake Vostok

Lake Vostok is about 250 km (155 miles) long and 40 km (25 miles) wide. It is completely covered by ice about 4 km (2.5 miles) thick. Underneath the ice is deep liquid water. No one is sure why the water does not freeze. The water is about a million years old. Scientists think it is the most unpolluted water on Earth. They want to study it to learn about life long ago.

Almost all of an iceberg stays below the sea's surface – only an eighth of the iceberg can be seen above.

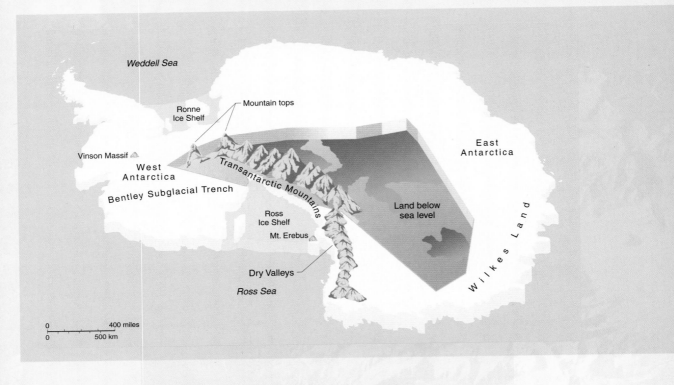

You can see how the land and ice in Antarctica fit together.

The mountains

You can see the tops of the Transantarctic Mountains peeping up through the ice. These mountains divide the continent into Eastern Antarctica and Western Antarctica.

The Dry Valleys

Just to the west of the Transantarctic Mountains, near the Ross Sea, lie the Dry Valleys. They were made millions of years ago when the mountains pushed up faster than the glaciers travelled to the sea. The glaciers got stuck on the east side of the mountains, away from the coast. The Dry Valleys are fields of bare rocks between the mountains and the coast. It is windy enough in the Dry Valleys to keep the snow away. No **precipitation** has fallen in over two million years! The Dry Valleys are classed as **deserts**.

The South Pole

Imaginary lines of **longitude** divide the Earth into segments like an orange. The lines meet at the North and South Poles. You can't see the poles with your eyes, so to mark the position of the South Pole, a 3 metre (10 ft) long stick is pushed into the ice. Because the ice sheet that is on top of the continent is always moving, the stick moves too. Over a year, it moves about 10 metres (30 ft).

Each year, the people who live at South Pole Station have a special ceremony to push a stick into the new spot on the ice that covers the South Pole. They leave the old sticks in place. You can see them stretching out, making a line that points to the coast.

ANTARCTICA FACTS

- *Thickest ice:* Wilkes Land — 2,900 m (9,500 ft) deep
- *Highest point:* Vinson Massif — 4,897 m (16,067 ft)
- *Lowest point:* Bentley Subglacial Trench — 2,538 m (8,327 ft) below sea level

WHAT IS THE WEATHER LIKE IN ANTARCTICA?

Summer and winter

Antarctica almost doubles in size in the winter. The continent itself doesn't change size – it grows because the sea around it freezes into **sea ice**. The ice grows from February, at the end of summer, until September, at the end of winter. By September, it has spread to cover about 20 million square kilometres (12 million square miles).

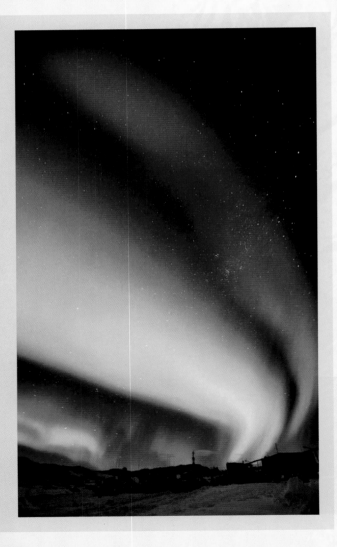

Cold and snow

All this ice makes it very cold in Antarctica. It gets colder as you move inland and as you move higher up in **altitude**. Eastern Antarctica is colder than western Antarctica because it is a higher **plateau**.

It is much too cold in Antarctica to rain. It is even too cold to snow very much. This means that Antarctica is a desert. At the South Pole, only 2 to 5 cm (1 to 2 inches) of snow fall a year. That is less precipitation than in the Sahara Desert.

The people who live at research stations in Antarctica have the best view of the Southern Lights. These are caused by particles in the Earth's atmosphere.

Antarctica is warmer at the coast. More snow falls there. Most snow in Antarctica doesn't melt, since it is too cold. Instead, it slowly packs down. As it sinks under new layers of snow, all the air is pressed out of the snow. Over thousands of years it is pressed into ice.

The wind in Antarctica is really fierce.

Windiest place

Antarctica is windiest near the coast. Even when snow isn't falling from the sky, it blows around the continent. It makes storms called **blizzards** and **whiteouts**. No one can see or do anything during these storms.

ANTARCTICA FACTS

- *Coldest recorded temperature:* Vostok Station, 1983: minus 89.2°C (minus 128.6°F)
- *Highest temperature:* Hope Bay and Vanda Station, 1974: 14.6°C (58.3°F)
- *Average precipitation:* 50 mm (2 inches) a year

Warming up

In the summer, Antarctica warms up enough around the coast for the sea ice to melt. Ice on the Antarctic Peninsula and islands also melts. Freshwater lakes form from the melted ice and snow. Plants and animals take the opportunity to breed and feed during the short summer.

The world's longest day and night

The sun only rises and sets once in a year in Antarctica. At the South Pole, there is a month or so of dawn while the sun rises above the horizon. For about six months there is almost constant daylight. Then a month of dusk leads to about four months of constant night.

For months at a time, the Antarctic horizon looks like this, with the sun set low in the sky, day and night.

WHAT PLANTS AND ANIMALS LIVE IN ANTARCTICA?

The **climate** in Antarctica is harsh, and there is little land exposed above the ice. This makes it very hard for life to survive there. Most of the plants and animals that live in Antarctica grow and breed as quickly as they can during the short summer sunlight. During the dark winter, they **migrate** or go **dormant** (a kind of sleeping).

Plants in Antarctica

Antarctica has a few land plants, which are mostly slow-growing and very small. It may take hundreds of years for a small group of **mosses** or **lichens** to cover a patch of rock.

The Antarctic Peninsula and islands have milder climates and deeper soil. More plants grow there, but they are still not very large.

Did you know?

In the Dry Valleys, there are some tiny plants actually growing inside rocks. There, they stay warm and out of the wind. Enough light reaches them through the rock to keep them alive.

Some **algae**, called red algae, grow on the snow during the summer. They stain whole snowfields red.

Tiny animals

There are only about 200 kinds of tiny insects and **invertebrates** (animals without bones) living in Antarctica. The biggest is 12 mm (0.5 inches) long! These tiny animals eat land plants and algae growing in lakes.

Krill are tiny invertebrates that look like shrimp. They live in the ocean. Krill are incredibly important to life in Antarctica. Most of the animals eat krill, from whales to birds to fish. Krill feed on algae and other very tiny plants and animals.

This is an Antarctic mite, magnified to many times its actual size. It is able to survive at extremely cold temperatures.

Life in the water

In Antarctica, the water temperature doesn't change as much as the temperature on land does. This makes it easier for life to survive in the water. The sea around Antarctica has a great deal of life in it. Some grows very slowly, just as on land. Sponges and coral live for hundreds of years. Small sea plants and animals, such as seaweed, crabs, and **sea anemones**, live near the bottom. Other animals, such as jellyfish, swim higher up.

Most of the animals in Antarctica have learned to live with the cold. Some, such as seals, whales, and penguins, grow a big layer of fat to keep warm. Others, such as some fish and invertebrates, have a kind of antifreeze in their blood, to keep it from freezing in the cold.

The biggest animals

The only really big animals in Antarctica are whales, seals, and penguins. They live mainly in the sea. Some live on land or ice for part of the year, usually to breed. They stay near the edges of the continent or on the Antarctic Peninsula and islands. They all rely on the sea for their food, and most of the big animals eat krill.

Killer whales feed on seals, penguins, and other fish.

Did you know?

There are about 600,000 billion krill in the ocean around Antarctica. Together, they weigh more than all the people on Earth.

Big babies and long lives

It is hard to breed and **rear** babies in Antarctica. This means that animals have only one or two babies a year, and they usually have very long adult lives. For example, emperor penguins live for 20 to 30 years but they only have one chick a year.

Whales don't breed in Antarctica. They have their babies in the warmer waters to the north. Some come to Antarctica in the summer to eat huge amounts of krill. Others eat seals and penguins.

The Weddell seal

The Weddell seal spends the winter mostly under water, where it is warmer than on land. But seals are mammals, and need to breathe air at least once an hour. So Weddell seals make breathing holes in the ice. They keep their breathing holes open all winter.

In the spring, Weddell seals go on to the sea ice to have their pups. After feeding them milk for six weeks, the adults teach the pups how to catch their own food in the sea.

Birds

Three types of bird breed only on the continent of Antarctica. Most make their nests on exposed land. Since there isn't much of this, most birds nest near the coasts or on the islands.

Adélie penguins make their nests from small stones. They nest in large groups. It gets very loud as thousands of penguins call to each other to find their families. The snow petrel manages to find quieter mountain ledges to build nests on, some 300 kilometres (185 miles) inland.

Some beaches are crowded with up to a million penguins all nesting together.

Did you know?

The colossal squid has the largest eyes of any animal on the planet. It can glow to light up the sea around it, which helps it find food. The biggest one ever found whole weighed 150 kg (331 lb) and measured 5.4 metres (17 ft) long. It was a young one, since the squid can grow to about 15 metres (49 ft) long.

The emperor penguin is the only penguin that never leaves Antarctica. It also never actually touches land, only ice.

The emperor penguin

The emperor penguin needs nine months to breed and rear its chicks before they are strong enough to survive. The summer in Antarctica is too short for this, so the penguins mate and lay their eggs on the ice before winter begins. Then the females go back to sea for the winter. The male emperor penguins wait on the ice, warming the eggs in a special pouch above their feet, during the two worst months of winter. They have no food.

By the spring, the ice has spread. The females walk up to 160 km (100 miles) across the ice, to arrive just as the eggs hatch. The females feed their chicks fish they ate at sea, **regurgitating** it into the chicks' mouths. The males walk all the way back to the sea to find their own food. Then they bring more food back for the chicks, and the females go to sea. They work like this until the chicks are big enough to go to sea and get their own food.

WHAT ARE ANTARCTICA'S NATURAL RESOURCES?

Raw materials, such as minerals, coal, and oil, can be found in Antarctica. The problem is that these **natural resources** are very far under the ice. Getting them out could destroy the environment. If they were mined, shipping them out of Antarctica to be used elsewhere would be nearly impossible. For these reasons, the 45 countries that have signed the **Antarctic Treaty** have agreed not to try. This agreement will last until 2041.

Living resources

The Antarctic Treaty countries have also agreed to protect the natural resources in the sea. In the past, some types of seals, whales, and fish were hunted almost to **extinction**. Today, there are strict limits on fishing and hunting. In Antarctica and the waters around it, killing or hurting any living thing is forbidden without a **permit**.

There are billions of krill in Antarctica. They are caught and used as animal feed. Because there are so many, a catch of about 1.5 million tonnes a year is allowed.

Whaling has strict controls to preserve the number of whales in the oceans.

19

Scientific resources

The continent of Antarctica itself is a huge resource. At the South Pole it is very dry and cold, and dark for six months of the year. There, astronomers can see space more clearly than from anywhere else on Earth. Other scientists are studying how the climate and **ozone layer** are changing.

Some scientists drill deep into the ice to learn about the Earth's past.

Did you know?

The early explorers and researchers in Antarctica used dogs to pull their supply sleds. But by 1994, people were beginning to understand how easy it was to upset the **ecosystem** in Antarctica. They agreed that animals that are not **native** to Antarctica would not be allowed there. This meant that all the sled dogs had to go back home. Now people use small tractors and snowmobiles with engines to get around.

ARE THERE ANY COUNTRIES IN ANTARCTICA?

When explorers came to Antarctica, they claimed land for their home countries. By the 1950s, seven countries had claimed land in Antarctica. All of the claims looked like pieces of a pie with the South Pole at the centre. Some of the claims overlapped others. Since no one lived full-time in Antarctica, none of the claims were permanently settled.

Changes and decisions

In 1957, twelve countries worked together on special science projects in Antarctica. They decided to ignore land claims because no one was going to make money from Antarctica's natural resources and no one was going to settle there permanently. All twelve countries, including the seven with claims, instead agreed to make it easier for scientists to work in Antarctica. They held 60 meetings and, at the end of them, signed the Antarctic Treaty in 1959.

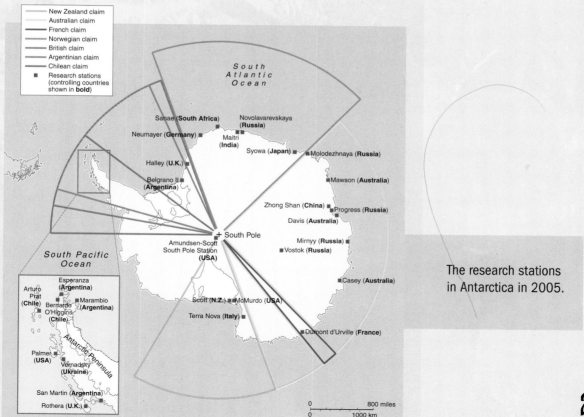

New Zealand claim
Australian claim
French claim
Norwegian claim
British claim
Argentinian claim
Chilean claim
■ Research stations (controlling countries shown in **bold**)

South Atlantic Ocean

Sanae (**South Africa**)
Novolavarevskaya (**Russia**)
Neumayer (**Germany**)
Maitri (**India**)
Syowa (**Japan**)
Molodezhnaya (**Russia**)
Halley (**U.K.**)
Belgrano II (**Argentina**)
Mawson (**Australia**)
Zhong Shan (**China**)
Progress (**Russia**)
Davis (**Australia**)
+ South Pole
Amundsen-Scott South Pole Station (**USA**)
Mirnyy (**Russia**)
Vostok (**Russia**)
Casey (**Australia**)
Scott (**N.Z.**)
McMurdo (**USA**)
Terra Nova (**Italy**)
Dumont d'Urville (**France**)

South Pacific Ocean

Esperanza (**Argentina**)
Arturo Prat (**Chile**)
Marambio (**Argentina**)
Bernardo O'Higgins (**Chile**)
Antarctic Peninsula
Palmer (**USA**)
Vernadsky (**Ukraine**)
San Martin (**Argentina**)
Rothera (**U.K.**)

0   800 miles
0   1000 km

The research stations in Antarctica in 2005.

All the countries that have research stations in Antarctica take part in talks about Antarctica. Any country that is part of the United Nations can also sign the Antarctic Treaty. New decisions about Antarctica have to be agreed by all the countries.

The Amundsen-Scott South Pole Station is run by the United States. It hosts scientists from all over the world. The stripy pole is the ceremonial South Pole.

Did you know?

On January 7, 1978, Emilio Marcos Palma was born on the Antarctic Peninsula. He is the first person in history to be born in Antarctica, and the only person in recorded history to be first-born on a continent. Emilio's parents were Argentine, so Emilio is a citizen of Argentina. His parents were living on a research station when Emilio was born.

WHO EXPLORED ANTARCTICA?

For thousands of years, people thought that there might be land at the southern end of the globe. In 1773, Captain James Cook sailed close to Antarctica, but didn't see land. Hunters started sailing to the area to catch seals and whales. In 1820, people set eyes on the Antarctic landmass for the first time. Over the next 90 years the land was sailed around and maps were drawn. By 1959, most of Antarctica was mapped.

The race for the South Pole

By the early 1900s, people started to compete to be the first to reach the South Pole. There were several brave attempts but most met with disaster. It was very difficult to dress properly for the extreme weather and to carry enough supplies. Food that kept people healthy, such as fresh fruit, didn't last in the extreme climate. Most of the early explorers died or had to turn back because of these problems.

On December 14, 1911, the Norwegian explorer Roald Amundsen finally reached the South Pole with four men. They got home again safely.

In 1915, Ernest Shackleton tried to cross the continent, but his ship, the *Endurance*, got stuck in ice. Over the next 17 months his team had to camp, walk, and sail in awful weather trying to get home. The story of their rescue is one of the greatest adventures ever told.

ANTARCTIC EXPLORATION

1773	James Cook sails near the Antarctic continent, but sees no land.
1819	William Smith finds an Antarctic island.
1820	The Antarctic Peninsula first sighted.
1821	John Davis is probably the first to land on the Antarctic landmass.
1830–1840s	The coastline is sailed around and it is proven that Antarctica is a continent.
1902	Robert Falcon Scott leads his first expedition to the South Pole, but has to turn back.
1907–1909	Ernest Shackleton's expedition to the South Pole gets further, but has to turn back.
1909	Douglas Mawson's expedition reaches the South Magnetic Pole.
1911	December 14: Roald Amundsen reaches the South Pole and returns alive.
1912	January 17: Scott's second expedition reaches the South Pole but the men die on their way back.
1914–1916	Shackleton's expedition to cross the Antarctic becomes trapped in ice and a heroic survival and rescue adventure takes place.
1935	Caroline Mikkelsen is the first woman on Antarctica.
1956	Plane lands at the South Pole – the first people there since Scott and his team.
1955–1958	Vivian Fuchs and Edmund Hillary lead a successful expedition to cross Antarctica.
1965	The first tourists visit Antarctica.

WHO LIVES IN ANTARCTICA?

No one lives in Antarctica for very long. The cold, altitude, and harshness of life are too much for people to survive, even with good shelter and food. The conditions are close to what it is like in space. Scientists study people's bodies and minds while living there, to try to work out how they would cope living away from planet Earth.

Scientists and technicians

Most of the people in Antarctica are scientists who come for the Antarctic summer that happens from October to March. Some people stay for the dark winter, to keep the research stations open. These people are electricians, doctors, cooks, and mechanics – only a few are scientists.

All the waste made on the research stations in Antarctica has to be taken off the continent. This means a lot of recycling in daily life.

Did you know?

At the South Pole, all the **time zones** in the world meet. So time zones mean little in Antarctica. Different research stations pick different time zones to use, often the same time zone as their home country.

Tourists

Each year, about 3,000 people visit Antarctica as tourists. They come to see the amazing ice and the millions of birds, seals, and whales. Sportspeople go climbing, hiking, camping, skiing, and scuba diving. But most of all, tourists come because Antarctica is such a wild and unique place.

Being there

In Antarctica, the only colours are blue, white, and grey. You can go for short trips in small boats, close up to the ice and water. You can get very near the penguins' nests. You can visit a research station, to see how people live and work there. They will even stamp your passport to show you've been to Antarctica!

Tourists can be taken in small boats to see the icebergs close-up.

WHAT FAMOUS PLACES ARE IN ANTARCTICA?

The South Pole

The most famous place in Antarctica is the South Pole. There is a special Ceremonial South Pole near the real South Pole. It looks like a barber's shop pole with a silver ball on top. It is surrounded by flags from all the countries that have signed the Antarctic Treaty (see page 22). People who visit the South Pole have their pictures taken here.

Mount Erebus is famous for being the world's southern-most **active volcano**. It is on Ross Island in the Ross Sea. The lava lake in its crater reaches temperatures of 1,130°C (2,066°F). The temperature on its slopes in the winter gets as low as minus 60°C (minus 76°F).

Ice shelves

The ice is so well known in Antarctica that the ice shelves are given names. When the water below and the air above an ice shelf gets warm enough, it breaks off into the sea. One of the biggest ever was the Larsen B ice shelf, which made a huge splash into the sea in March 2002. It was 2,717 square kilometres (1,049 square miles), which is half the size of Crete in Greece!

CONTINENTS COMPARISON CHART

Continent	Area	Population	
AFRICA	30,365,000 square kilometres (11,720,000 square miles)	906 million	
ANTARCTICA	14,200,000 square kilometres (5,500,000 square miles)	officially none, but about 4,000 people live on the research stations during the summer and over 3,000 people visit as tourists each year. People have lived there for as long as three and a half years at a time.	
ASIA	44,614,000 square kilometres (17,226,200 square miles)	almost 4,000 million	
AUSTRALIA	7,713,364 square kilometres (2,966,136 square miles)	approximately 20,090,400 (2005 estimate)	
EUROPE	10,400,000 square kilometres (4,000,000 square miles)	approximately 727 million (2005 estimate)	
NORTH AMERICA	24,230,000 square kilometres (9,355,000 square miles)	approximately 509,915,000 (2005 estimate)	
SOUTH AMERICA	17,814,000 square kilometres (6,878,000 square miles)	380 million	

Number of Countries	Highest Point	Longest River
54 (includes Western Sahara)	Mount Kilimanjaro, Tanzania — 5,895 metres (19,340 feet)	Nile River — 6,695 kilometres (4,160 miles)
none, but over 23 countries have research stations in Antarctica	Vinson Massif — 4,897 metres (16,067 feet)	River Onyx — 12 kilometres (7.5 miles) **Biggest Ice Shelf** Ross Ice Shelf in western Antarctica — 965 kilometres (600 miles) long.
50	Mount Everest, Tibet and Nepal — 8,850 metres (29,035 feet)	Yangtze River, China — 6,300 kilometres (3,914 miles)
1	Mount Kosciusko — 2,229 metres (7,313 feet)	Murray River — 2,520 kilometres (1,566 miles)
47	Mount Elbrus, Russia — 5,642 metres (18,510 feet)	River Volga — 3,685 kilometres (2,290 miles)
23	Mount McKinley (Denali) in Alaska — 6,194 metres (20,320 feet)	Mississippi/Missouri River System — 6,270 kilometres (3,895 miles)
12	Aconcagua, Argentina — 6,959 metres (22,834 feet)	Amazon River — 6,400 kilometres (4,000 miles)

GLOSSARY

active volcano volcano that erupts regularly

adapt learn to live the best way possible in a certain environment

algae tiny plant or plant-like living things

altitude how high up something is above sea level

Antarctic Treaty agreement made between many countries about how to manage and protect Antarctica, first signed in 1959

blizzard storm with strong, very cold winds and fine snow, which makes it hard to see

climate how hot or cold, wet or dry, and windy or still a place is

continent largest land mass on the globe

desert place where very little rain falls year round

dormant alive, but only just – not active or alert

ecosystem all the plants and animals and the environment they live in, that use and depend on each other to survive

environment place where a plant or animal lives, and how wet or dry, or hot or cold it is

equator imaginary line around the middle of the globe that divides north from south

extinction when the last of a whole type of living thing dies

glacier frozen slow-moving river which drains water from high up down to the sea

ice sheet thick layer of ice over the ground

ice shelf thick ice which floats on the sea and is joined on one side to an ice sheet

iceberg big chunk of melting ice that breaks off glaciers and ice shelves and floats into the sea

invertebrate animal without a backbone

landmass big area of land

lichen small plant made when algae and fungus grow together

longitude imaginary lines that run from north to south around the Earth, dividing it into sections like an orange

migrate to move from one place to another

moss tiny plants that grow like tufts

native people, plants, or animals that are the first to live in a place

natural resource material found in the Earth and sea that is used to make other things or for food

ozone layer part of the atmosphere that reaches almost all around the Earth and blocks out the sun's harmful rays

permit agreements that allows a person or company to do something that is restricted, such as hunting or polluting

plateau raised, flat area of land, sometimes high up

precipitation water falling from the sky, as rain, snow, ice, or hail

raw material the basic ingredients that are used to make finished goods

rear to raise babies until they are old enough to survive on their own

regurgitate to swallow food and then bring it back up into and out of the mouth when it is needed, usually to feed babies

research station place designed and used for scientific research

sea anemone small animal with tentacles that is often bright colours so it looks like a sea flower

sea ice ice that forms on top of the sea. It isn't salty, since the salt is pushed back out into the water below when the ice freezes

tabular shaped like a tabletop

time zone the world is divided into sections, like an orange, and each section has its own time zone so that the sun is directly overhead at noon in each time zone

whiteout when everything around you goes white during a blizzard so you cannot see anything except white

FURTHER INFORMATION

Books

Ann and Liv Cross Antarctica, Zoe Alderfer Ryan & Nicholas Reti (Da Capo Press, 2003)

Life in the Antarctic (Biomes), Lynn M. Stone (Rourke Publishing, 1996)

Antarctica (Continents), Jane and Michael Pelusey (Chelsea House Publications, 2005)

Antarctica (True Stories), David Petersen (Scholastic, 1999)

Discovering Antarctica series, June Loves (Chelsea House Publications, 2002)

Hooray for Antarctica! (Our Amazing Continents), April Pulley Sayre (Millbrook Press, 2003)

March of the Penguins, Luc Jacquet (National Geographic Books, 2005)

My Season with Penguins: An Antarctic Journal, Sophie Webb (Houghton Mifflin Company, 2004)

Trial by Ice: A Photobiography of Sir Ernest Shackleton, Alexandra Shackleton (Foreword), K.M. Kostyal (National Geographic Books, 1999)

Useful websites

- British Antarctic Survey site, with a special section for schools. Excellent questions and answers about daily life and scientific work:
  http://www.antarctica.ac.uk/Resources/schoolzone/index.html

- Archives of the *New South Polar Times*, the South Pole newspaper:
  http://205.174.118.254/nspt/index/index.htm

- Centre for Astrophysical Research in Antarctica has a kids' page with experiments and great information:
  http://astro.uchicago.edu/cara/southpole.edu/

- *The Antarctic Sun*, the United States Antarctic Program's newsletter:
  http://antarcticsun.usap.gov/2005-2006/sctn06-21-2005.cfm

- This is a site full of general info about Antarctica and about travelling there:
  http://www.antarcticconnection.com/antarctic/info-index.shtml

- The Mount Erebus Volcano Observatory website has lots of information and great photos:
  http://www.ees.nmt.edu/Geop/mevo/mevo.html

Disclaimer

All the internet addresses (URLs) given in this book were valid at the time of going to press. However, due to the dynamic nature of the internet, some addresses may have changed, or sites may have ceased to exist since publication. While the author and publishers regret any inconvenience this may cause readers, no responsibility for such changes can be accepted by either the author(s) or the publishers.

INDEX

Titles in the Exploring Continents series include:

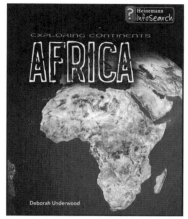

Hardback   0 431 09742 9

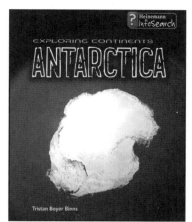

Hardback   0 431 09743 7

Hardback   0 431 09744 5

Hardback   0 431 09745 3

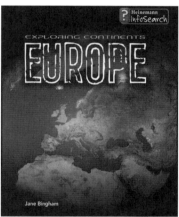

Hardback   0 431 09746 1

Hardback   0 431 09747 X

Hardback   0 431 09748 8

Find out about other titles from Heinemann Library on our website www.heinemann.co.uk/library